YOU AND WHAT ARMY?

Redefining Self and Community

I0445318

Dr. Jesse Sanders, Ph.D.
Dr. Matthew Wilmot, Ph.D.

RALEIGH, NORTH CAROLINA

Dr. Jesse Sanders, Ph.D., Dr. Matthew Wilmot, Ph.D.
Rain Publishing, LLC.
PO Box 14397
Raleigh, NC 27620
www.rainpublishing.com

You and What Army? / Jesse Sanders, Matthew Wilmot.
-- 1st ed.
ISBN 979-8-9855005-0-9

Library of Congress Control Number: 2021925475

CONTENTS

INTRODUCTION

This book will support individuals and families in our community and those whose common goal is to uncover the root of oppression and redefine their identities through positive, inclusive, and expressive means. We want to help those who have been oppressed self-realize and self-actualize their life on their own terms and be able to find their identity and purpose.

"You're now permitted to explore"

Part One

WHAT'S MY IDENTITY?

By Dr. Jesse Sanders, Ph.D.

ME, MYSELF, AND I

I remember like it was yesterday. I was sitting in my upstairs bedroom window on 14th Street, waiting to go to church - the one and only New Light Missionary Baptist Church. I was in elementary school. Momma Vida is what some of us called her. She was everything to the young people. I remember many moments. I loved going to church, I loved connecting with the people in the ministry. I loved the moments when the spirit moved. It hit the most intimate parts of me, the parts that no one had access to but God. The painful section, the perplexed section, and the relinquished section.

No one could direct a choir like Aretha Williams! Such passion, knowledge, ease, and yet such strength for music and direction. And when Chad Walker struck those keys on the organ or keyboard it was over! Do you hear me? Over! Pastor Bachelor would get up and minister with fire and then always remind us of how Jesus got up on the third day. Those were the moments that I began to cognize my distinctiveness.

I had the best of both worlds because I also attended and was a faithful member of New New Bethany Church of God In Christ (C.O.G.I.C.) under the leadership of Elder Edward Rice, a man that did not accept any mess and refused to operate in chaos! My aunt Elaine was a missionary, and I would ride with her. She was the epitome of an amazing graceful, strong, and beautiful woman! I know those genes came from the apple of my eye, my grand-mother. I LOVED the Pentecostal flow with the music, the tongues, the dancing, and the altar calls with fire! It was so awesome because New New Bethany C.O.G.I.C was in the same jurisdiction as my great-aunt's church, Thompson Memorial C.O.G.I.C, under the leadership of Evangelist Evelyn Thompson. She served until her transition in her 90's.

It was there my cousins and I were able to grow our gifts, we were able to sing, we even formed a group; I have pictures to prove it. I remember Kesha hitting soprano notes and those faces Fremont, Freeman, and I used to make when we felt that song in our belly. My cousin Fremont, who is also like my brother, and I were also able to sharpen our ministe-rial gifts there. Those were some fun and glorious times!

Although those were some fun and glorious times, there were some tumult moments as well. My father passed away when I was a child, and my biological mother had some unstable moments in her life, as we all have. As a result, I moved in with my grand-parents when I was in middle school. I still held on to the belief that there was something incomparable about me. But I couldn't completely visualize it as I went through life's detours.

I must admit, my life was not unpleasant with my grandparents, although they were still not my parents. My grandparents were the template of what a healthy family should emulate. They worked together as a team, supported people that were not within their bloodline, those individuals and family units that considered them parents and grandparents. I can't count the number of headaches people gave them, including myself. Throughout my life lessons, their integrity, wisdom, love, and words are always a guiding light, which is unrivaled. My grandmother was and continues to be the apple of my eye. She is the epitome of what a virtuous woman is, even when she had to get us together!

Although I had a great life with my grandparents, and nothing can be taken from the seeds that were deposited into me, I wrestled at times with what I knew was in me and what I witnessed around me. I am speaking in an all-inclusive tone. Every vision and dream that was in me, I did not see it that big around me. Therefore, at times I toiled with the strategic plan of manifestation. Also, my biological mother and I rebuilt our relationship, and it was healthy and enjoyable until her transition in December 2018. Although the journey was not one that I would have constructed, I enjoyed our ride of laughter, support, and robust love.

Because there was no blueprint for who I knew I authentically was, I rammed numerous brick walls. When we struggle with our innermost self, it costs, and the price is excessive and unjustifiable. We pay emotionally, financially, spiritually, and yes, even physically. It diminishes us to a lesser individual. Trust me, I have paid the price in each of the aforementioned areas. I had to learn to create my destined reality, remain focused, utilize the power within me, and continue to gain traction, no matter the conditions that were placed before me.

I remember the first day I made a conscious decision to not only become the change but to become the trailblazer for my family. It was September 21, 2000, my oldest daughter Brianna was born, I looked at her cute rosy cheeks and her beautiful innocent face. I was reminded at that moment, "I am responsible for another person," a person that did not request to be here, but she was. I remember making a covenant with God that I would not be or become the dysfunction I witnessed in so many. I wanted her to see and experience different. That is one of the primary reasons I fight so hard for family units today, because of that day. Her mother and I had to co-parent; we were still a family unit. Therefore, every decision I made, was made with love and wisdom for my daughter, as I know the feeling of not having active parent(s).

I believe both parents are equally important, therefore selfish motives or unhealed hurt was not going to, nor should it be for any parent an active position in effective child-rearing. The second time, the covenant to continue to be the change, was when my Little Momma, Brielle, was born in 2009.

Another life I was responsible for, and she would be looking towards her mother and me for protection and proper fostering. I can certainly say, I am grateful for this co-parenting unit because we have changed the rules of the game in our network by allowing others to see that you can have a healthy, integral, and happy parental relationship, in two separate homes. I contribute a great portion of Brielle's "Little Momma's" emotional healthy and vigorous individualism due to Tresia and I creating a methodical and wholesome environment.

Moving forward, I remember sometime later in my life I desired to have some questions answered regarding my father, who is a part of my identity. I had faint memories of him, and I have heard people speak of him, but there were still pressing questions. There I was standing in the store and this woman was continuously staring at me. Then she approached me and said, "Excuse me, may I ask your name? I think we are related." I merely laughed, because I can remember from an early age, people telling me I am my father's twin, from head to toe. She then began to tell me that I have more family, including a stepmother in the same city. In the same week, a woman told my ex-wife the same thing and I began to think, "Finally, my questions can get answered."

I remember uneasily dialing my stepmother's telephone number and she was expecting my call. I remember asking Tresia, "Do you think I should meet with her?" She responded, "You have been desiring some answers, what harm could meeting do?" That was some of the best advice because I met her that week. When I met her, I remember talking for hours, looking at photos, and getting my questions answered. I found out I had another brother, Terrence. He found out I was there, and he came immediately after work. It was amazing and fortifying. I had another family structure entrenched in my life. It was one of the best liberating and transformative moments in my life. From that moment, I met my sister Jean, my sister-in-law, brother-in-law, nieces, and nephews. Some people ask, why was that moment of meeting Mom Freddie, my stepmother significant to me? The response is simple, it met a need that was imperative to me and my journey!

Of course, there are many moments I have engaged in, in my life. However, some are monumental. Another momentous moment is the night I met my awesome sisters, Brandy and Precious shortly after I relocated. The next day, after meeting Brandy we talked on the phone for hours, as she was traveling back to her home state to visit. The connection was most certainly a God connection. Through my relationship with her, I have learned a lot about living an authentic life, making mistakes, complete ownership, vulnerability, and much more! That is one of the many reasons I value that relationship and you will never hear me say, that she is "like" my sister. She is my sister! We have taught each other so much and have fired each other more times than we can count, but we are still rocking strong together.

There is more information that I will share in future writings with many more people in my life I love and cherish. However, the aforementioned information I have shared with you is vital. As you prepare to engage in this reading, you will understand some of my heart, some of my story, and my objective.

The objective is to explore the concept of identity and the ways it impacts individuals and families. Education is key to understanding what identity means, first at a personal level, then at a more global level. Challenging the status quo is also crucial to help shape an individual's or family's views on who they are or what they believe in. Finally, redefining an individual or family's relationship with themselves will help them understand their place in the world. Ultimately, understanding one's identity can help one find their place in society - something that can be beneficial and liberating.

In discussing identity, we will be challenged to become a redefined individual and/or family unit, uncovering the root of oppression, and redefining our identity through positive, inclusive, and expressive means. The goal is to help those who have been oppressed self-realize and self-actualize on their terms and be able to find their identity and purpose.

When we rob ourselves of tunneling deep to identify and grow in our authentic self, we rob ourselves of exploring. We are our inventors, authors, and power beings. We have the powerful privilege to write and amend our life stories. We do not need anyone else to tell us how to live. We can construct the life we aspire for ourselves, with the people we love, converting our dreams into our reality. There is no such thing as limits, but we can still block ourselves from our greatness when we are afraid of the unknown and uninvited pressures from society.

Our culture shapes the way we process and perform, and it influences how we visualize ourselves and others. It affects our values - what we believe to be correct and wrong. The society we sleep in often affects our choices. But our choices can also influence others and help define our community.

Imagine that we meet a stranger while walking down the street. How would we describe that person? Which label would we use? We all know that each person differs in countless ways, yet once we meet others, we often rely on generalizations to explain them.

Through its culture, customs, institutions, and much more, our society provides us with the labels used to classify the people we encounter. These labels are supported beliefs about race, ethnicity, religion, gender, sexual orientation, economic class, and more. Sometimes our beliefs about these classifications are so unswerving that they prevent us from seeing the unique identities of others. Sometimes these beliefs make us feel doubt, fear, or hatred towards certain members of our society. Other times, especially once we are ready to understand a person, we're prepared to look past categorizations and get a foothold.

There's a term in sociology called racial identity development, and it describes the process people of color go through when they attempt to understand and embrace their racial and ethnic heritage.

I cannot allow my being to be dictated by what I've been preconditioned to be by circumstances, culture, and more. If I were to ask myself if it is right for me to be uncomfortable or if it is right for me to feel shame because of who I am, the answer is no. However, somewhere along the way, I have learned to embrace this idea. I have learned to accept cultural norms due to my incapability of defying them.

You may have heard the expression, "if we can't think for ourselves, at least do our best to think differently." What does this expression mean? "If we can't think for ourselves…" conveys that if we are unable to think for ourselves, we are relying on our environment to think for us. The phrase, "think differently," instructs us that if someone has deemed us incapable of thinking for ourselves, then at least try to view events from another perspective.

Everyone has not made the conscious decision to think for themselves. Some people have allowed themselves to become an adversary to enlightened progressive thinking. Sometimes this is due to situational factors, sometimes it's due to social pressures, childhood trauma, and occasionally it happens because of race or gender.

When we start something new, we have a lot of questions to ask ourselves. For example, when we start a new business, we must identify who will be our clients and determine what type of products or services our clients require. When we have a child, we must decide how we're going to provide for that child and exhibit principled standards. When a relationship begins to progress, we must ask ourselves if it has sustainability and what kind of future we desire from it.

In these moments when we decide to think about what kind of situation we find ourselves in, the question is, "What do I think about this?" Questions like this can be helpful in problem-solving or in determining what's going to happen next in a situation.

However, what happens when the next thought is a question? This would be a great time to ask, "How do I think about this?" This is where the importance of reflection and critical thinking is applicable. Critical thinking is the ability to make sound judgments and come to valid conclusions by using logic. With critical thinking, we can learn to understand, evaluate, and act on information in ways that are based on facts rather than emotions.

Critical thinking requires us to be skeptical, open-minded, logical, rational, objective, and ethical when determining what information is accurate or inaccurate. Critical thinking is one of the basic skills necessary for all human beings to survive, whether in business or personal life.

When it comes to critical thinking, not all people are parallel; some are more skilled than others. Those who are skilled in critical thinking will naturally be able to make better choices, apply reason to solve issues, resolve problems, or produce innovative solutions. Critical thinking is a skill that can be learned by anyone regardless of age, gender, or experience. The ability to use critical thinking skills commences at home with the way parents raise their children.

The art of thinking is a common misconception, and we need to reconsider the idea of what thinking is. We all think we know what it means to think, but it's not until we are reminded of our thoughts by someone else that we realize how many assumptions are made. Our understanding of who has access to this "art" varies depending on how we configure our life. It's not always an easy task to think for oneself if we've been conditioned to function with limitations.

Some people have opted to accept their way, while some want more than they have, and some want less than they have. The more control we have over our thoughts, the more we can change our reality. What happens when we allow people to place us in restraints?

Oftentimes, we ask ourselves the question, "Who am I?" The answer to this question is one that constantly evolves. It is, rather, something that changes from time to time. When we consider who we are, we often refer to certain factors that have influenced who we believe we are. Some of these factors often refer to backgrounds, personality traits, interests, belief systems, moral code, and experiences. But what exactly is our identity? What are the factors that build up the identity we associate ourselves with throughout our lives?

I believe that all the things we do, the type of choices we make, the decisions we choose to avoid, everything is influenced by our perception of our identity and how that identity interfaces with society. While this may be good to an extent, a number of the factors that influence our identity can serve as limitations to true self-discovery and living a liberated life.

ONE

WHAT DOES IDENTITY MEAN?

Before we can consider the factors that influence and limit our identities, we must first consider what identity means. So, what does identity mean?

According to the Merriam Webster Dictionary, identity is defined as:
- "The distinguishing character or personality of an individual."
- "The relation established by psychological identification."
- "The condition of being the same with something described or asserted."
- "The sameness of essential or generic character in different instances."
- "The sameness in all that constitutes the objective reality of a thing."

Each of these five definitions provides insight into five different viewpoints of the term 'identity.' Most individuals have an identity within themselves that is based on the way we have identified ourselves psychologically. However, personality traits and distinguishing characteristics that influence our identity are objective to us and subjective from the perspective of others in our immediate society. We may identify ourselves as being trustworthy or confident, while others in society may regard us as unreliable or arrogant. This presents two dimensions to what identity is – personal identity and social identity. Though both are intertwined, I will focus more on personal identity and the factors that can serve as limitations to living a liberated and purposeful life.

Identity is shaped by the process of socialization, which is a lifelong process that shapes individual identities into society's expectations. Identity is not static- it shifts and changes over time.

The process of socialization can be broken down into three stages: primary socialization, secondary socialization, and tertiary socialization. Primary socialization occurs in the home during childhood, while secondary socialization occurs in a school or on the job. Tertiary socialization takes place when an individual encounters new people with different beliefs and ideals.

CHILDHOOD TRAUMA

Childhood trauma or developmental trauma is one of the most common factors that strongly influence our identity as individuals. It is even more common than most of us seem to realize. According to an article by the National Child Traumatic Stress Network, before they clocked 5, 78% of children had reported experiencing trauma more than once.

People who suffered developmental trauma are likely to develop cPTSD or Complex Post Traumatic Stress Disorder. Some of the major characteristics of cPTSD include difficulties in areas like memory, consciousness, emotional regulation, and self-perception, which particularly affect how we identify ourselves and can limit us from living a meaningful life.

Formation of identity is an integral aspect of human development, and it takes place as a continuous process, starting from birth, through childhood, adolescence, then adulthood, and finally senior age. Our identity is responsible for our sense of being good enough, our integration of intellect and emotions, our awareness of various emotional states, our feeling of coherence and security as individuals, and our experience of who we are. All these are disrupted when developmental trauma develops. This is often because our basic survival instincts are prioritized and the resources that should have fueled normal self-development get exhausted in the process. Childhood trauma causes a shift in the trajectory on which normal brain development moves upon. This is because the presence of certain factors in our environment causes the brain to adapt by taking countermeasures off its normal path. For example, if a person grows up in an environment majorly characterized by neglect and fear, our brain is more likely to adapt in several other ways than feeling safe, secure, and loved. The earlier in life that the trauma occurs, the more significant the effects tend to be, on average.

Being able to develop our identity as an adult is a challenging yet rewarding experience. However, the process can be particularly distraught for people struggling with the aftereffects of childhood trauma. Our identity development and consequently most parts of our lives get stuck because of the aftereffects of childhood trauma, which most times includes depression, eating disorders, substance abuse, behavioral issues, difficulty in professional development, and difficulty in creating or maintaining personal relationships.

The identity development of a person that is addressing unresolved childhood trauma often revolves around being a survivor and the maintenance of basic safety when compared to other people. This typically leads to disheartening repetitions and re-traumatizing which can hinder growth-oriented experiences. Individuals in this condition often tend to identify with the "traumatic self" as opposed to a sense of self that is more inclusive and amendable. In cases where an individual experiences significant childhood trauma, it is usually customary for us to experience alienation from ourselves and our environment.

Below are some of how unresolved childhood trauma influences the identity of a person.

· Missing childhood memories

People who experienced a lot of distress during childhood are often unable to remember huge portions of their childhood. Sometimes they may experience flashbulb memories. That is when they recall memories that are vivid but usually the memories they recall lack context. They tend to lack the storyline of their childhood through other developmental stages. The absence, underdevelopment, or oversimplification of this coherent narrative makes a weak foundation for developing one's identity.

· Incomplete sense of self

Dissociation is a common coping mechanism for people who experience childhood trauma. This makes people who experience distress at an early age heavily rely on a major persona and portray themselves in that light as though everything was fine. Thereafter, they may feel as if they are incomplete.

· Being drawn towards destructive relationships

Several people who were traumatized by their caregivers often find themselves in friendships, relationships, and work settings that are not healthy. It is possible to often get into relationships with people who have similar trauma profiles. Usually, these individuals may be narcissistic, abusive, or emotionally unavailable and when there is a repetition of the experience that was encountered, they become re-traumatized.

When a person who suffered trauma as a child continually ends up in destructive relationships, they tend to become disoriented and confused, and they begin to question their self-understanding. This cycle locks them into their old identity and prevents them from forming new identities.

· Avoiding relationships

People whose developmental trauma involved intimate relationships may choose to avoid relationships and prefer to remain in isolation. For some people, this may start early while for others, it may start much later as a means of breaking the cycle of unhealthy relationships they may have been struggling with. However, healthy relationships form a crucial aspect of identity development, as they present numerous opportunities for change and growth. Avoiding them further affects the process of identity development by solidifying a personal perspective of unworthiness.

·   Difficulty regulating and integrating emotions into one's identity

When they grow in an environment where feelings are absent, their emotions are usually separate from their identity. This causes them to have an unpredictable sense of self especially because they cannot control their strong emotions. This situation is regarded as emotional dysregulation and it leads to consequences from making impulsive decisions as they require their emotional data to make conscious decisions as themselves. It also hinders the formation of healthy relationships.

Fortunately, it is possible to work on the trauma identity one has assumed from experiencing distress during their childhood. You can create a healthy identity as an adult. Through therapy and a few other conscious steps, it is possible to address those pain points so that you can go on to develop a healthy identity for yourself.

THREE

MENTAL HEALTH SEQUEL

Mental health is also a factor that can strongly influence the identity of a person. When your mental health is decontaminated, you can go through identity development competently. If otherwise, you may find identity development a lot more challenging, and your mental health matter may serve as a limitation to living a fulfilling life. Mental illness can and will even override a person's intellect. I will touch on two major areas where mental health issues can create difficulties with identity development.

· Low Self-Esteem

Low self-esteem is basically when a person has a poor sense of their self-worth. It occurs when you begin to believe that you have little or no value and worth. Oftentimes, this is a result of being constantly criticized by key people in your life. It could also be a result of being a perfectionist. Most perfectionists are usually critical. In any of these cases, there is a tendency of judging yourself harshly. You are also likely to ignore or downplay the importance or value of your accomplishments, even though there is no rational explanation for doing so. In a different scenario, you may hold the belief that your self-worth is based only on the acclaim or opinion of other people of "high social status," even when this is not true.

· Low Self-Efficacy

Self-efficacy is a term used in describing the level of effectiveness and control you believe you can exercise over your lives. Everyone needs that feeling that makes you know you control certain aspects of your lives. This feeling helps you to proffer solutions to difficult situations you find yourself in and to face challenges you are expected to encounter. When a person feels helpless and cannot change the negative situations that they may find themselves in, there is a tendency that they will battle depression. This situation of feeling helpless in such circumstances is regarded as learned helplessness.

Indeed, you cannot control every aspect of your life. However, there are several remarkable areas that you have the power to influence. People who battle low self-efficacy have low expectations of themselves and this causes an individual to believe that they are helpless and unable to influence any area of their lives. And even when such persons may be suffering, they tend not to try to make any changes to the situation. In most cases, self-efficacy is specific to certain domains, so one might feel in control of some areas of their life and may experience a feeling of helplessness in some others.

Mental health issues affect virtually every area of an individual's life, causing reduced and slow development in our academics, professional, social, and even personal life. On the bright side, these issues and several other mental health issues that may exist can be addressed and managed effectively to enhance growth in affected areas and consequently identity development.

FOUR

RELIGIOUS BELIEF AND REDEFINING RELATIONSHIP

Our experiences and environmental areas are crucial in forming our beliefs and influencing our identity. Beliefs that receive wide acceptance become a part of the culture and they influence the society we primarily live in.

Of all belief systems, religion is about the most dominant of them all as it has existed for many years. In several ways, some have utilized it to serve as a rule book or code of conduct designed to guide the ways a person functions and interacts with the rest of society. The earliest forms of religion that existed were set up to enable social bonding with like-minded individuals. It is also generally believed that practices of these religions were adaptive and have gradually evolved. Also, many have formed their own personal relationship with the Creator and believe they must, "Study to shew thyself approved unto God, a workman that needeth not to be ashamed, rightly dividing the word of truth."

It is then not a surprise that religious systems are essential to our thinking patterns and play a crucial role in the development of self-identity and even the common identity of communities, as they go on to shape the values, attitude, and cultural norms that influence the behavior of individuals and groups in the society. The influence of religion is stronger on children because they are more easily susceptible to accepting the explanation of a phenomenon that emphasizes purpose rather than cause. These beliefs are held strongly even into adulthood. Factors that contribute to this include the belief in God's existence, His omnipresence and immortality; the ascription of certain psychological qualities like compassion, fairness, and harshness; and the ascription of His involvement in the lives of individuals.

Some religions that exist today compel moral behavior from believers using positive and negative reinforcements with 'God-fearing' concepts infused into their respective scriptures. These concepts include reincarnation and karma in Hinduism; hell, and paradise in Islam; salvation, Heaven, and hell in Christianity; and reincarnation and the peaceful afterlife in religions indigenous to the Chinese. All these beliefs in the supernatural being capable of rewarding and punishing people compel a certain behavior in them.

While religious systems may be a good thing, they can also be limiting. The fear of what the supernatural can do may hold us within a mental cage and prevent us from living an authentic liberated life, incorporating wisdom, of course. That fear may also prevent us from exploring certain areas of our lives that may enhance our growth and develop our identity as individuals.

In a world that is constantly shifting and redefining terms, there is a growing number of individuals who have chosen to stop identifying with religion and have chosen to embrace a relationship with God instead. The prevalent behavior in today's society is driven by the idea that people understand God from their own experiences, not by what has been relayed to them by religious doctrines. This is nothing new; however, what is new is the willingness of people to be more open about their outlook on spirituality. An example of how people are behaving towards spirituality can be seen in the growing number of people who claim no religious affiliation. The percentage of adults who do not identify themselves with any particular religion has steadily increased in recent years. From 2007 to 2014, the percentage of religious "nones" increased from 15 percent to nearly 23 percent.

In conclusion, currently, we have found ourselves being able to relate to God as we gain knowledge and wisdom. In other words, we have been able to establish a personal relationship with God. This is important because no one should have to conform to a standard that is imposed by others. People should not feel dictated to feel any certain way or be required to adhere to certain standards or even doctrines that others would like them to follow in the name of religion. That is why many people have a personal relationship with God and a strong resolve not to allow religion to dictate what they do in their own private lives. It is not my intention to create religious rebels. However, I am intentionally establishing a safe and truthful space provoking us to embrace authentic relationship versus religion.

FIVE

HOW TO EMBRACE OUR UNIQUENESS AND IDENTITY

Having an identity that is built majorly on negative influences can make one feel flat, frustrated, and unfulfilled. However, that is not the end of the road. It is always possible at any time to develop a better and clearer identity of oneself and be able to live one's best life. This process, though, may be challenging, especially for persons who experienced distress earlier on in life, but it can be more rewarding if they can successfully pull it off. The following steps can be taken to heal and set forth on the path of a redefined journey.

· Define your values

Values and belief systems are integral aspects of identity development. Having a belief system helps us to recognize the things that matter the most to us and help to determine our stance on crucial issues.

Values help us set boundaries we establish for ourselves and our relationship with others and help us pilot these boundaries. For example, if we are a person who values honesty, we would find it difficult to continue a relationship with a person who hardly tells the truth.

We don't need to define all our values at the same time, it is a development process. We can build on the basics as time goes on.

·   Take charge of your life

As an individual, you must learn to take control of your life in areas you can control. In those areas, you need to take charge and make decisions that are up to you to make. In making those decisions, you should consider your well-being and health, and then the people you might be accountable for, for example, your child or partner.

In the past, you may have left vital decisions in your life to other people to make. This may make taking charge seem difficult and intimidating but it is not. Simply, start the process. Do things because you want to do them, not because of anyone else.

This does not mean you should not seek guidance from people. Seeking assistance is a healthy thing to do. But it still boils down to us to make the decisions that affect you.

·   ·Get to know yourself

If you wanted to know someone, you would spend some time in their company, right? Well, the same applies to getting to know yourself. You would need to spend quality time alone and take moments to deflect. This is not to say you should isolate yourself. That would be unhealthy. Instead, you should have alone time when you can truly discover yourself.

It is up to you to decide what to do with this time. However, I can suggest that you try out new hobbies, read more books, volunteer, meditate, or keep a journal.

·   Plan towards your ideals

When you have an ideal self in mind (who you see yourself becoming) and there are differences between that and who you currently are, there is the tendency to get frustrated and even depressed.

This may cause a feeling of emptiness and can affect your self-esteem, thus, preventing you from developing your identity.

To bridge this gap, you can make visible plans towards your ideal self if it is a realistic possibility, or you can consider changing such ideals if they do not seem feasible.

THE SELF AFFIRMATION THEORY

I want to talk with you about the power of self-affirmation. When we create affirmative actions, we must form affirmative words. We become what we consume. Therefore, I charge you to reflect on what you have consumed and what you desire to consume. Operate in the realm of reality and not delusional creativity.

This is a technique that can be used to make life adjustments and create the life you want on your terms. Sometimes, you get stuck in life. You don't feel like you are living your best life or even worse, you don't know how to move forward with your life because you are paralyzed by fear or some other limiting belief. That's where self-affirmation comes in. Self-affirmation exercises can help you change your mindset and start taking steps towards living the type of life that you want to live - one that is on your terms and one that makes you happy!

Self-affirmation is an empowering process.
We all have regrets. We can't reframe our past, but we should use this time to create an environment where it is easier to thrive.

You should consider that the way you are living your life, your decisions, you're your actions are what determine how you will be remembered. So, before you go out there and try to change who you are, take a moment and think about whether this will be an improvement for yourself.

Only when you have lived your life the way you wanted can you say that you have truly lived at all.
Affirmative action is a change in plan. Change is the only thing constant. But if we're going to forge ahead, we must change the way we think and view things.

The responsibility, of course, is ours because we're the only ones who can do it. We're the only ones who must do it. It's not someone else's job to change our life. It's ours. In addition, we must understand that this responsibility is permanent and ongoing. We can't just do it once and never worry about it again. It's a process.

I'm not going to get too deep into this, but I had a conversation with someone the other day and I realized that I've had a lot of conversations like this one.

When it comes to our lives and the direction we're taking and the journey we're on, we talk about how difficult it is to get where we want to go. Many of us have become so comfortable in our discomfort and dysfunctional circumstances/relationships and while we acknowledge all our struggles and while we see the roadblocks every step of the way — we simply think — that's just what it is. However, in our new course, we must understand, affirmative actions and affirmative decisions can turn the tides.

I'm committed to always looking at my life as a work in progress. I understand that I will make mistakes and that change can be a difficult thing. I understand that a paradigm shift is a major event in the life of a person and that choosing to change the things that need changing, is a decision that some people will never make. If no one told us, it's okay. It's okay to be who we are even if we cannot define who we are now.

Remove yourself from those who try to define your sanity based on your circumstances. Take a mental break from those who don't believe you, and from those who errantly assume you should live a life that supports or addresses their needs. Take a mental break from those who think they know everything but know nothing about the cost of a commitment to inconsistency.

SEVEN

GETTING SUPPORT/THE PARTNERSHIP

The process of identity development can be quite overwhelming and challenging, particularly if you have never given much consideration to your identity.

As the journey can have its moments of uncertainty, you will feel overwhelmed, mystified, and stuck. That is why it is crucial to reach out to a therapist or any other mental health professional for help. Therapists can help you overcome problematic and developmental matters, such as depression, low self-esteem, low self-efficacy, persistent frustration and unhappiness, anxiety, and other factors that could arise.

Even if you do not have any symptoms of mental health issues, you can still consider therapy as a good place to start your identity development.

Getting into therapy can be particularly helpful for persons who experienced trauma in their childhood and are affected by PTSD (Post Traumatic Stress Disorder). Other mental health conditions that may hinder proper identity development like histrionic personality disorder, dissociative disorder, border-line personality disorder, and schizophrenia can also be treated in therapy.

While it has become more commonplace for conversations on mental health, there is still some pervasive stigma around seeking help for issues (which is not unpredicted).

CONCLUSION

Wisdom has been considered an art that most have had to seek out. This quest for knowledge is rooted in human nature. As most of us are curious about the world, we desire to gain information on the mechanics of it so that we can work with what was given to us. We are the only beings in the world that know about ourselves. It is this desire to know ourselves that leads to our pursuit of wisdom.

Not only will wisdom positively impact our lives, it gives us the ability to also harness knowledge and thinking to understand ourselves. Through others' individual stories we can relate to each other, and rich conversation creates a bridge between people so that we can discover a much better understanding of life and the people around us. When we change the questions we ask, we can change the way we think, and by changing the way we think we can change our life.

Now, I will admit that I am not some all-knowing wise person, but I do pride myself on accumulating knowledge that is relevant to my health and enhancement. My grandparents made certain that wisdom would be applicable in my life, and I am eternally grateful.

The concept of identity is not easy to grasp or understand because our identity evolves and develops over time with every phase of life we go through. Also, as we have learned, there are many contributing factors regarding the dynamics of our identity.

There are times you may experience moments of self-doubt or confusion. Those are typical moments. However, if you constantly struggle with a feeling of emptiness and frustration, you should consider taking time for self-discovery and getting professional help from a therapist. In doing so, you are accepting responsibility and accountability. Also, you can correct certain factors in your life that may hinder your identity development.

If you're going to make progressive changes, it is of the utmost importance that you utilize wisdom. Wisdom is a linchpin of happiness and purpose in life. It is the key to making sense of all the confusing information you are bombarded with today, to make better decisions and feel more at peace with how you live an enlightened and redefined life.

In a TED Talk, Sir Ken Robinson said, "I believe creativity, at its essence, is a way of seeing." And that is exactly what we want to do for ourselves. We want to see things in a different way that will change the way we live our life. We see a world where people aren't judged by their gender, race, ethnicity, religion, age, etc., but by who they are as human beings.

We see a world where people feel secure and assertive in being their true selves without being condemned and instructed to change or be molded into someone else's unrealistic programmed individual. We see a world where individuality is encouraged so we can all see more of who we are. We see a world where we have clearance to be ourselves, on our terms and our tempo.

The world needs us to be our authentic selves! We were created in the image of our Creator to convey who we genuinely are into the world.

Questions:

1. What negative and/or positive impacts that have been conditioned by society and culture affect my life?

2. How can I change my identity to better fit my goals?

3. What are the ways that childhood trauma shaped my identity?

4. What are some ways that I can cope with past trauma?

5. What does it mean to live my truth and authentic life?

6. How does living my truth and an authentic life make me feel?

7. What are the benefits of living my authentic life?

8. What are the challenges of living my authentic life?

9. How can I live my truth and an authentic life daily?

10. What are the benefits of living a life without regrets?

11. What are the steps for living a life without regrets?

12. Why is it important to have an emotionally healthy inner circle?

13. How does an emotionally healthy inner circle help with productivity?

14. What self-affirmations will I create?

Part Two

REDEFINING COMMUNITY THROUGH RESPECTING DIVERSITY

By Dr. Matthew Wilmot, Ph.D.

INTRO

If diversity is the mixtape of a community, inclusion is each song's runtime.

Diversity is a concept of understanding the differences in our environment that we perceive and communicate through our senses. Inclusion is the respect we afford to these differences through the way we attend to them. Our journey towards establishing acceptance within our community often begins with little room for diversity. We are frequently compared to a standard (or model) of virtue, even if we come from a less reputable community. This standard is seen as the pinnacle of what many in our community deem the best and brightest. The standard can be both material (suburban house), personal (cis-heterosexual, male), or conceptual (Christianity). In consequence, our strivings to match this standard often require an agreement with the community to limit our identity expression and, thus, fall in line with our neighbors, relatives, and friends. From as early as childhood, this agreement is made, often without much conscious awareness. To come into our own and affirm ourselves, separate from the agreement we make with others, the previous section highlights that we need to embrace the constancy of change.

Within our communities, we have norms of behavior that are formed based in part on some combination of the way we interpret laws set by an institution (e.g., government), our perception of that institution, and our perception of each other. These factors can affect our attitude and behavior towards diversity. The latter is what we define as the level of inclusiveness. When we negatively respond to diversity, we justify our behavior via the belief that diversity is threatening the status of the community. As a consequence, we limit our inclusivity by either actively shunning (anger) or passively avoiding (fear) the others in our social spaces.

I'm here, both as the voice you are employing to read this part of the book and the very words on the page, to tell you that it is not our fault. You can breathe a sigh of relief. Historically, our communities have lived in a system bereft of the skills for managing diversity. Whether you are reading this in the United States, Canada, the United Kingdom, or elsewhere, in the past, we sucked, we have sucked, and we currently suck. However, it is our responsibility to change the way we perceive inclusivity so that we can benefit in the areas of our community that matter most to health.

As a social psychologist via doctoral training, I have come to view identity as a product of both context and person. The latter, however, can be substituted by community for the purposes of this part of the book. What I have learned from my tenure in this area of study is an understanding that it is less important for us to understand what identity is (person and context) but rather when identity is revealed. That revelation comes when we foster a spirit and environment of inclusiveness. It depends on times and places that produce a spectrum that spans from limited to limitless diversity. Affirming our collective involves recognizing the moments where we act in opposition to diversity and then engaging in a radical acceptance of a changing definition of what is normal and what is "deviant." In my not so humble opinion, deviance often is the product of dissonance, when we behave or think in ways that contradict values of diversity, inclusion, and pedagogy.

French psychologist, Jacques Lacan, once penned the phrase "I think where I am not; therefore, I am where I do not think." At first glance, this quote creates the image and feeling of curiosity in its delivery. Its play on a Descartes's inductive expression of existence ("I think; therefore, I am") is seductive in its appeal to us, considering how context can define a person. However, I believe that Jacques Lacan is providing a new understanding of space by asking us to consider if a space where we do not have to think is indeed "safe". A safe space must not only be physically safe but also identity safe. But the notion that being in a space that is identity safe should cause us to think less of our identity feels counterintuitive. I would like to think about the presence of my identity when I occupy a welcoming space. Therefore, I search for a space where I currently am not present (i.e., "I think where I am not") and welcome others who are not in my space. However, if I believe that my identity and, by extension, my community feels safe not having to always think about identity, then "I am where I do not think" may be safe.

To parse the significance of Jacques Lacan's quote and give a preamble into what this part of the book will be about, I have created two models to help us compare and contrast two ideals of identity-safe environments to test their validity. The gatekeeper model is formed to conceptualize "I am where I do not think", and the coordinator model, is formed from "I think where I am not". While being upfront, I strongly favor the coordinator model, I will lend a degree of freedom for us to consider the application of both models towards key indicators of community health.

When we consider the validity of coordinated identity-safe spaces, we resist the systems of oppression that create a certain standard of community. When we create gatekept identity-safe spaces, we place restrictions on our admission of others into the community. This gets expressed via holding signs that say, "I don't mind if you're [insert identity], as long as you stay in that section of the community," the subtext of these signs reflects the concluding phrase from the quote by Jacques Lacan. Drawing arbitrary lines in the sand which do not allow for exploration of self-critical thought can create a false sense of comfort through our traditional understanding of community. After all, idle minds are the devil's workspace. We do not have to think of the spaces where we are not present. The spaces where we are can become guarded by what I like to call the "terms and constrictions" of community.

What are these "terms and constrictions"? This was a question I began to ask myself while growing into my adolescent identity and continued to reflect upon in young adulthood. The answer became apparent when I accepted myself as a first-gen, Jamaican LGBT, Canadian-educated cis-male Doctor of Psychology currently transplanted in Ohio and a monogamous interracial romantic relationship, just to name a few of my intersecting identities. I began to see my national, gender, sexual, and relational identities as being the children I needed to take care of whose growth would not occur if I and others placed terms and constrictions on them. For me to balance my service to the community and service to myself, I had to understand when I was solely feeding one identity to the detriment of others. By extension, we can begin to remove these terms and constrictions and address crucial community goals through our cognizance of whom we are selectively feeding even in diverse communities.

I hope that we will work together to reveal examples of terms and constrictions that channel our thoughts, attitudes, and behaviors when respecting diversity becomes our goal. The puzzles and writing prompts I have selected, with much gratitude extended to the psychologists whose research created the space for me to articulate my use of their theorizing on human social behavior via these exercises. These prompts and puzzles will help you to unpack your perspective and compare it to the answers we suggest fit the mold (based on empirical work). Wherever you are in your attitude about community, I implore you to still complete them. This is meant for us to lay a foundation where we can begin to discuss how we work together to build a system of values that helps us 1) cope effectively with the institutional and intergenerational trauma that sometimes manifests itself in our perception of community, 2) develop a stable process of networking with each other to learn and understand our diversity, and 3) control the narrative we construct of our community so that others do not.

IMPRESSION FORMATION

Activity #1

In this activity, you will be presented with a row of three words that have some association with each other. In the line next to each triad, please write the word you think connects the two. For example, the words cat/carbon/right would be associated with each other through the word copy.

dew/comb/bee   _____

cracker/fly/fighter _____

pie/luck/belly _____

dust/cereal/fish _____

home/sea/bed _____

cross/rain/tie _____

mouse/bear/sand _____

Upon completing, how difficult was this activity?

_____

_____

_____

_____

Some of these word triads may have had multiple answers while other triads had a clear-cut solution. How enjoyable was this activity? Why or why not?

_____

_____

_____

_____

_____

_____

_____

Thank you for completing this activity. You can breathe a sigh of relief now. The purpose of this pre-liminary exercise, termed the Remote Associates Test by Drs. Smarnoff and Martha Mednick, were to demonstrate the efforts we go through to make com-mon sense of seemingly unrelated things through a creative answer. Psychologist Dr. Jean Piaget re-ferred to this tendency as schematic formation. It can also be referred to as convergent thinking. When we peer behind the mind's curtain, we can see that there is a process of redefining the meaning of one, two, or maybe all three of the words grouped together before we arrive at a solution. We implore some mental effort or brain grinding to accommodate the varying definitions of each word to find some overlap. There are varying degrees of difficulty in detecting the overlap because we can't just lump the words together without considering their unique references.

Just like how it was easy to complete some of the triads and difficult to complete others, so is the process of how we redefine our social surroundings. Recognizing our differences just as much as our commonality can be difficult. It takes increasing effort to remove dysfunctional habits of interpreting what community means and that includes discounting the belief that community is a group of individuals who conform to a uniform lifestyle. In the previous exercise, when you figured out the common tie between the three words, this didn't signify to you that the words have lost their original meaning. The words can still retain a common thread while also having the distinctiveness of being their own. Renowned psychologist Dr. Marilyn Brewer referred to this as a theory of optimal distinctiveness that people strive for. Distinctiveness is essential to expanding the ability of community to control our destiny through redefinition.

When it comes to redefining community through the respect we give our differences, it's easy. The first step is to profess our unconditional acceptance

of differences and their value insofar as those differences provide unconditional acceptance of us. It
almost sounds like the Golden Rule but it's not. Instead of solely treating others how we want to be
treated, consider also treating others how they want
to be treated. In the United States, we have been,
how shall I put it lightly, restricted towards treating
differences in physical features (e.g., darker skin),
behavior (e.g., sex work), and connectedness (e.g.,
transgender heterosexual polyamorous relationship)
with disdain and avoidance. These origins of the way
we perceive the different facets of our community often become the source material from which cultural
values and ideas are created and reinforced. For example, though most Africans living in the US are
numerically descendants of slaves brought via the
Middle Passage, a wealth of identities have existed
since the dawn of slavery and have continued to di-
versify through social interactions and making
meaning of one's existence. We're at a point in the
process of redefining community in families, workplaces, friendships, and community because we
have opportunities to interact with people from different places and times. Workplaces are becoming
increasingly diverse in terms of nationality (e.g., African, Hispanic, East Indian, Caribbean, e.t.c) and
age, some containing at least four different age gen-
erations (e.g., boomers, millennials, Gen X, Gen Z,
e.t.c). Rather than exclude what or who isn't "us," the
journey of a thousand miles toward redefining community starts with the first step of acknowledging that

you have placed terms and constrictions on the diversity of your community at one time or another and that you are able to commit to unconditional acceptance of diversity. It can be as easy as writing it down or just saying it aloud to yourself. Say it, right now! There! You're on your way.

Answers to the Remote Associates Test

dew/comb/bee ___honey___
cracker/fly/fighter ___fire___
pie/luck/belly ___pot___
dust/cereal/fish ___bowl__
home/sea/bed ___sick___
cross/rain/tie ___bow___
mouse/bear/sand ___trap___

TWO

THE PARADOX OF GATEKEPT DIVERSITY

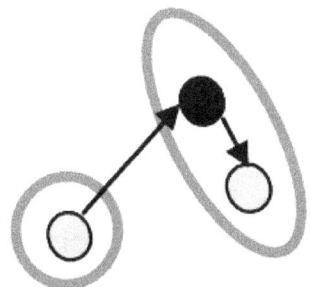

Gatekeeper

The test of a commitment to an unconditional acceptance of diversity is valid and necessary for community health if one is to measure the use of power to enact positive change. The power to enact change is often but not limited to a numerical representation of diversity because there can be unhealthy boundaries placed even on the disproportionate large populations. Committing to an unconditional acceptance also requires a pedagogical demonstration of the normalcy of diverse experiences and, thus, multiple standards of authenticity.

The gatekeeper paradox is the barrier to authenticity that can affect how a community responds to the opportunity for growth and prosperity. For example, an opportunity can be presented between the community and an organization that provides resources for community members. In this situation, the community may choose not to invest time in partnership because they believe that partnering with this organization would contradict the identity the community has established within itself. The community may make this choice as a collective or through people who are de facto gatekeepers of its reputation. Here is where the paradox comes in.

If you are a security guard at a nightclub and your role is to decide whom to let in and whom to turn away, there are two ways in which you can make a mistake. You can let in a person who shouldn't enter the club and you can turn away someone who should enter the club. So, what do you do to minimize mistakes? Well, that depends on what you prioritize. For example, you may prioritize solely based on physical appearance or whom people are connected to. These priorities require a review of what has happened in the past. You may prioritize appearance because, previously, you let in too many people who were not qualified, and it cost the reputation of the club. Your boundaries were loose or, unfortunately, violated at the time.

This may call to mind what we read earlier in Part 1 on childhood or adolescent trauma and the countermeasures we take to overcorrect for the risks we bore. These measures soon become norms that are created to understand our collective identity. We designate gatekeepers who create a standard that they believe will uplift the status of the collective and be our source of authenticity. But status doesn't equal power if our boundaries are only further restricted by the people we try to avoid or, comparably worse, the people we only gravitate towards. The paradox of gatekept diversity is that even when we make decisions to accept diversity, we can allow trauma and a false sense of unworthiness to prevent it from being authentic and creative.

During my formative years of growth and development in Toronto, I had to contend with the existence of different enclaves where my identity would come up against the social norms of my peers. Though I grew up in a Protestant Christian household, I attended a Catholic elementary and high school system that, while more accepting of students from other faiths (students who identified as Hindu or Buddhist attended), had a different set of unwritten codes of conduct. While emphasizing my spiritual identity (believing that we are all on a journey of progression guided by a higher power) appeared formidable in sheltering me from what were often contentious debates on the veracity of one's denomination, this method often prevented other identities from their full expression (i.e., my queerness, my Jamaicaness, my Protestantism). Though I found moments of expression during my years in high school and college, I eventually had to accept the paradox that is the rarity of power given to all my identities despite my belief in their existence.

We can apply this paradox to understanding the way folks in the community can often take great strides to police the space they define as acceptable. For example, instead of adopting an open mind about what Blackness is, we limit Blackness to the hetero-normative, masculine form that reflects the structures of oppression they were meant to guard against. We make strides to become sentinels of our collective consciousness and to influence the criteria for what defines community. We can engage in a process known as identity bifurcation, a concept penned by psychologist, Dr. Emily Pronin. And while her research on this concept was focused on bifurcation within persons, I believe that we reproduce this tendency via the ways we have gatekept the diversity of our communities.

Further perpetuating this paradox, we create social structures for how to best gatekeep diversity. These structures are dressed up as ad-hoc diversity committees, diversity enclaves (e.g., women's group, African American group), or diversity plans based on how we are conditioned to see diversity at its core, as a highly selective popularity contest. Paradoxically, these social structures of diversity were created for the benefit of White men and women, no matter their other identities (e.g., socialite, working-class, or newcomer). So, most who are vetted into a system of diversity, even if from a new group, are there insofar as they do not upset this social structure. That is the paradox of approaching our community from the position of a gatekeeper. We reproduce the system to the benevolence of its original beneficiaries.

Activity #2

In this activity, here are some topics that our community places strict gatekeeping rules on. Beside each topic, write a number that ranks it from 1 (least) to 5 (most) guarded.

__ family structure
__ physical health
__ income and wealth
__ gender and sexuality
__ mental health

Based on the rank order, explain why you ranked #1 to be _____. Explain why you ranked _____ at #5.

_____
_____

THREE

COORDINATED BLACKNESS

What is a coordinator? A coordinator is a person, community, or entity that works with two or more separate groups to call attention to overlapping means to a shared goal. The roles of a coordinator include but are not limited to a) the direction of parties to available and relevant resources, b) the equitable delegation of roles and responsibilities towards the shared goal, and c) the adjustment of means used by its partners towards the shared goal, based on a change in environment. To be effective in this partnership, a coordinator must show awareness of the shared goal and of the diverse ways to reach that goal. Both skills require the adoption of an inclusive mindset of all participating parties and their unique experiences.

Rather than simply acknowledge that diversity exists, coordinated diversity makes difference the default and equity the common goal. Instead of shunning differences, we can strive to ensure that different individuals in our community are empowered through working with each other towards the goal of redressing unearned power imbalances. We can venture from acknowledging difference to striving for equity by acknowledging that respect should be our priority.

As shown in the diagram, though all three actors are circles, one actor differs in color from the other two. Let's say, for example, the colors represent identities. The arrows represent the relation and potential for information to be provided. The lighter circle whose arrow is pointing to the darker circle is providing information. The lighter circle whom the darker circle's arrow is pointing to is receiving information. According to social network analysis, and research, it is believed that the ties to a common actor can increase the likelihood that the two actors will meet. In other words, the darker circle coordinates information to increase the likelihood that the two lighter circles will share information. The result is a triad of connections. The darker circle (the coordinator) is responsible for coordinating the information so that the triad forms.

What separates the formation of a coordinated (versus gatekeeper) system is the value placed on the prospective connection between all three actors. In the above diagram, all three actors are circles, but there is variation in color and connectivity. Despite this diversity, the large circle that encompasses the actors represents the common goal of equity as well as the collective that a coordinated system creates. The circle and oval that are depicted in the gate-keeper diagram represent a divergence in goals, values, and ideas such that there is no collective formed amongst the three actors.

Consider whether your family unit or community sees itself as composing one of these two systems. Chances are that we have learned to adopt a gate-kept system for the majority of our existence or we fluctuate between the two systems. However, if we are to unleash the power that makes us unrelenting in our pursuit of justice, we need to embrace diversity through a coordinated system of community. That is the task that communities will need to embark be-cause there may need to be a change in what is believed, valued, and beneficial.

Here are three steps on how to start developing your skill as a coordinator:

Practice removing your definition of "deviance" as solely a response to trauma and encourage others to do so. The word "deviance" was forced upon us by media, literature, and quasi-scientific analysis that sought to impute character flaws in people from marginalized groups and to punish those from privi-leged groups for not fitting a certain mold (e.g., cisgender, heterosexual, and monogamous).

Read literature or watch media on intersectional-identity experience both within and outside your social space of influence. Some examples are Janet Mock, Austin Clark, and Nicola Abraham, just to name a few. I trust that you will find others.

Contact a friend, acquaintance, or family member who is of intersectional-identity experience. This can be based on their professing of intersectional experience. Ask them if they would be willing to share their story about journeying towards self-discovery. Listen to it without expressing judgment and try to think about how similar your journey could be to theirs. Often, we try to construct the intersections we share with people by trying to assimilate them into our mold. Instead, exude deference by imagining where you are in their experience.

The more we start to redefine diversity in our communities, the easier it will become for us to witness the difficulties that our members struggle with personally. We can approach their experiences with an open and willing demeanor that will support our brethren towards the solutions that work. Diversity in gender, sexuality, economic means, and perspective has always been at the foreground of attempts to make progress in equity and will continue to be as people recognize their potential and overlap their visions with those around them.

In the following two sections, I will begin to compare and contrast the ways we apply the two forms of diversity (gatekeeping and coordinating) and their health consequences. This approach will help us witness the limitations that lie in the gatekeeper model and where the benefits are in a coordinated model. If there were a time to articulate a benefit of a gatekeeper model of diversity, I would think this is the time. A gatekeeper model appears to be efficient and often responsive to immediate threats to group solidarity, especially when there is a recognizable trait common to its members (e.g., dark skin, language/lingo). It can feel akin to a fight-flight-freeze response, which is effective in the short term; but afterward, harmful.

Therefore, as we cover the sections that are titled based on the forms of health, consider their importance to the survival of our community and, thus, are areas of diversity for us to improve. They are physical environment, gender, and sexuality.

ENVIRONMENTAL HEALTH

Community is a construct of people and places that interact through mutual and complementary relationships. As a child growing up in a diverse and middle-class residential area, I saw the prosperity of my mental health as tied to others through the outdoor environments we shared. The neighborhood offered a multiplex of social interactions that ranged from the comfort of driveways, the nearby soccer field at the elementary school we all attended to the forested areas. Though I didn't think much about my identity within the different spaces, I came to appreciate them more when they were no longer available and what was left were memories. These spaces were a canvas of social creativity where the children of the neighborhood, hailing from Caribbean, Italian, Chinese, Portuguese, and East Indian families congregated to define themselves.

These spaces often start as liminal spaces - the unoccupied driveway, the playground, the forested areas. Liminal spaces are areas that have an undefined purpose but signal an impending transition. Think of liminal spaces as a waiting line, the one we all love to be in at the checkout. In these spaces, time can sometimes be perceived as moving slowly. For some, it can feel like those who are occupying this space are standing in the way of a transition. But for those who have an appreciation of the environment, their identity (whether personal or communal) is inextricably linked to the prosperity of the outdoor space.

Historically, Black and Indigenous communities of color (BIPOC) have had to deal with the ephemeral emotion of fear and the chronic expression of anxiety towards spaces that are portrayed as liminal because of the racist projects that serve to displace them. In an article, I wrote recently for PsychReg, BIPOC communities that contain forests, waterways, and the diversity of flora and fauna are under attack by forces that replace natural landscape with "squeaky clean" parkettes and small ponds that are encapsulated by unaffordable high-rise condominiums and strip malls that displace families. This form of replacement deals a huge blow to the wonderful diversity we often take for granted.

A reduction in the biodiversity of BIPOC outdoor environments can compromise the connection these groups have with nature, a connection that dates back several millennia. I symbolized this relationship as that of a securely attached, parent-child interaction where give and take to benefit both parties exist. When we begin to replace this environment with something that feigns resemblance but stymies connection, we are geriatrifying (i.e., placing Father/Mother Nature in a "nursing home" for them to be rendered invisible) spaces of connection to this greater entity.

The relational identity that we have with our biosphere is connected to the identity we ascribe to our community of people, and this predicts how we will respond to its changes. These responses are often personal and caused by fear of removal and a perceived lack of control over the changes that are occurring. When those changes do not align with our connection to the biodiversity of our environment and, more importantly, our values, we feel less in control and may try to regain it Malcolm X style, by any means necessary.

Our responses are also collective because we recognize the power of shared fate in places where identities are included in the conversation to reconnect with the Earth. While this can be seen as universal for all people, regardless of identity, it is primarily evident in the philosophy and culture of African people across the diaspora. Terms like Ubuntu (I am because we are), Imani (faith in the collective), and Umoja (unity among others) embed the self in a network of relations. Consequently, how we respond to our local biome will be informed by our trust in what those near us will do. But what does the collective do? What they do falls along the spectrum of gatekept vs. coordinated diversity.

I stayed home and commuted via public transit to school during my first two years of college. In my third year, I bought a car and decided that it would be easier to commute to school using my car. My family and I added justification to the purchase by reasoning that it would be a time saver and easier on the environment if I bought a Honda. We often sorted our trash, recycled, limited intake of red meat, and used our utilities to the bare minimum of sustainability. However, when I eventually realized the painstaking effort to maintain the car I had, it felt as though the practices of conservation were futile in comparison to the non-renewable resources my car was using up. I had no issues with public transit that warranted the use of a car in the first place.

In retrospect, I did not align my value of the environment with the values inherent in my other identities. I saw being Black as not related to being conscious of my environment and the practices I could take and encourage others to take. My Blackness, my queerness, and other elements of who I am were not inclusive of the possibility that I could commit myself and, to a certain degree, my family and friends to becoming environmentally conscious.

Often the extent to which we commit our practices to partner with Father/Mother Earth to ensure mutual sustainability is governed by whether a person and their community see this as part of the pinnacle of their identity. If you recall, gatekept diversity is the restriction on what is allowed to be considered diverse. In the space of environmental health, it is what we choose to see as "our" environment-sustainability practices. Often we select what is simple in order to abide by a norm that is set for us by institutions or we refuse to commit altogether because it doesn't seem part of the culture (e.g., vegetarianism is White people stuff even though historically and even today, the African diet is vegetarian). Not surprisingly, our simplicity yields few gains in the fight to stop institutions from producing the waste we are trying to eliminate. We limit our notion of diversity in the realm of environmental health to simple practices while eschewing other behaviors that may inconvenience us. Consequently, we may fail to appreciate the intersection of environmentalist identity with other identities.

Gatekeeping diversity has been demonstrated in the realm of environmental health by the priority placed on leading the agenda on environmental sustainability. Because a community agenda that seeks to reclaim our connection with Earth requires foregoing immediate personal benefits in the service of long-term collective benefits, there is often little incentive to expand our collective identity to include environmentalism. The protected standard of diversity is often limited to that which brings riches and wealth. This standard is especially present when embedded in a capitalist society. Changing that standard would require a re-evaluation of those whom we deem the "cream of the crop" in our society (e.g., multi-million-dollar people). Those who occupy this esteemed category are sheltered, for now, from the effects of impending environmental shifts due to climate change. That's probably why, for example, seldom will one hear African American individuals in positions of power and influence discuss publicly their support for environmentalism. If they do publicly express support, they rarely convey the effort to address the environmental impact of their often-multiple dwellings. The absence of their articulation on the subject matter influences our attention to it and the inclusion of environmentalism on the diversity agenda.

How do we change from applying a traditional gatekeeper tendency to a coordinator tendency? What is the advantage of applying coordinated diversity to environmental sustainability? I will start by answering the second question first. Recall that the advantage of coordinated diversity is to allow for information to flow between recipients in the network that is encompassed by a shared goal. When we apply coordinated diversity, we are affirming a sense of respect we have towards each other for the paths we took to reach this point of intersection. The parties involved trust that the coordinator is delivering information that strengthens their bond and pulls curiosity in the direction of learning other's unique features. When we approach diversity as a tool for generating creative solutions that address pressing issues, it reinforces the intimacy of working together even when we may understand a problem differently. Coordinated diversity will expand our definition of community to include the treatises of environmentalists and the historical connection we have with Earth. We will be empowered through this approach because we recognize that we are part of something greater than our individual pursuits toward monetary wealth.

The interconnectedness of us and nature is a reminder of the nonjudgmental places on Earth where we can find solace. There are members of our community who are aware of this and seek within themselves to commit to an environmentalist way of living. However, they are often kept out of the limelight because of reasons such as fears of mysticism communicated by conservative religiosity, less access to healthy food dieting in poor communities, or lack of comprehensive education on the subject matter.

Based on these reasons, it appears simple to dictate how we change our community from being gatekeepers to coordinators. A coordinator would communicate the plan and strategy for us to change our perception of these barriers so that we can incorporate an environmentalist agenda into our plan of diversity. However, even that step is difficult because of how ingrained some of these factors are within our communities and existing sociopolitical systems. It will take relentless action to become an effective coordinator. Effective coordinators must display the capacity to leverage relations. Usually, coordinators differ from both parties in a system of social relations and can take a more objective and integrative position. They can piece together gaps as a way to demonstrate the potential benefit each party has to the other.

When coordinators elucidate the potential benefit of collaborative work between unacquainted groups, communities will elevate their skill at identifying with all forms of diversity. Members will be able to assist in projects that require interdependence and fulfill identity-related goals. In the realm of environmentalism, this is a form of diverse identification that appears new to many within our community. While gardening and farm development are commendable, this work is often localized and personal. This work resonates with a neoliberal philosophy of natural resources that prioritizes individual behavior to reduce waste rather than a collective action to protect, grow, and incorporate the largest swaths of our community's natural landscape. The benefits of these personal behaviors are often diminished when larger institutional projects, led by multi-billion-dollar entrepreneurs, invade our space and erase our efforts.

To resist these forces, we must start with including environmentalism as part of our identity, regardless of where we are in life. As mentioned in part 1, identity is not fixed nor stable when there are a multitude of ways we choose to make certain parts of ourselves salient. We can make our identification with environmentalism salient through education on what factors must be considered when we are at the table with land developers, zoning officials, and other organizational leaders that make decisions on our property. Additionally, we can support environmental entrepreneurs, especially those from communities most impacted by climate change.

We need to act collectively to replenish forests and natural landscapes that are often infringed upon by well-meaning, yet ignorant public-private infrastructure plans trying to clean up markers of "physical disorder". We have the diversity and the coordinator potential to begin to think about investing in the engineering of environmentally efficient housing and outdoor recreational spaces from plastic and cardboard wastelands, subsequently replacing those wastelands with greenspace. Our historical connection with nature can inform the direction in which we harvest from Mother/Father Earth to sustain our tribes and, at the same time, remain stewards of its prosperity. An example of this translation of connection to direction is in the Rastafarian ecological ethic that views nature just as much the object of our responsibility as our source of vitality (which they famously term itality). The mutuality inherent in this agenda and its individuality, via removing the "v" in vitality to focus on the "i", with which this connection allows nature to be a continuous source of life aligns with a coordinated approach to diversity.

If coordinating diversity towards improving the environmental health of communities still seems foreign or unattainable, you may be right. When there is social pressure to behave in ways that reinforce gatekeeping, it can draw pessimistic expectations. Diverse and practical methods are often met with resistance, especially when it requires us to put in more effort and time than is convenient. It is seldom endorsed by the materially successful people and organizations they represent. Like starting a business, the costs of coordinated diversity may outweigh the benefits at first. It may take more convincing than is worth the time. If you and others are reading and discussing these issues in synchrony, then the value of environmentalism as a diverse part of our rooted village will potentiate to empower our other identities.

The costs of pivoting toward coordinated diversity can be borne immediately, and they include adjusting the standard of living that many of us have grown accustomed to seeing via the perks of capitalist greed. When we pivot toward a coordinated form of diversity, we can begin to witness what equity looks and feels like no matter the position that a person occupies on the socioeconomic ladder. Under this model, equity will be clearly defined so that those most disenfranchised will begin to envision the prospect of prosperity. Prosperity may not feel the same as what we are accustomed to seeing through a capitalist lens. A coordinated diversity model will require a redefinition of the term, one which may have already existed but has eluded our gaze for quite some time. However, our acceptance of this new definition will prove beneficial to the long-term health of our communities.

Activity #3

In the space below, provide a reason why we need a Black-focused plan for addressing environmental health.

_____

_____

_____

_____

_____

_____

_____

_____

Describe a plan that will help you and others become comfortable having a conversation on environmental health. This plan can include panel discussions, demonstrations, training, etc.

_____

_____

_____

_____

_____

_____

_____

_____

_____

_____

GENDER CARE AND SEXUAL HEALTH

In an earlier part of this book, we defined what identity is and how its definition can help us comprehend its development and its self-serving function. While identity can be understood as a tool for excavating beneath the surface of just living, it is effective in recognizing both the points whereby we intersect with others (via shared identities) and points of parallelism (via unshared identities). What is unique about parallelism is the extended opportunity it creates for holding mental space. This mental space, which may occur within and between persons, invites a positive redefinition of others through mutual respect. When you commit to understanding different others as being just as much a point of reference for the community (shared mental space) as yourself, you can begin to appropriately minister to their needs.

In this section, let us delve further into understanding how coordinated diversity can help us see the value of identity variability in two areas of health that have recently exemplified its promising application to need ministry: gender and sexual health.

Gender-related health typically centers around the human body and the impact that external circumstances (i.e., poverty, system anti-Black ideology, and food insecurity) have on the organ systems. The usual suspects who rule this topic with a (quite literal) iron fist are the "cardiovascular crew" and the "digestive dynasty". These often lay claim to our attention as the prime physical markers of our gender-related health, with infrequent glances at the importance of reproductive health. While these markers garner benefits through committed attention, our over-focusing on them can often set priorities in the favor of cisgender people.

We must understand that the intersection of racism and sexism on the health of many underserved identities has percolated spaces in order for us to redefine the construct of gender within our lifetime. We are now becoming more attentive to the fallacy of gender being a binary system. Even more, the gender binary system may be just as significant a contributor to topics we discuss in other health domains. This historic error in judgment of gender has served to erase the health concerns of certain gender groups that do not appear to "fit" the mold of what is a woman or a man. Notably, many persons in these groups identify as African or Hispanic transgender persons, those who identify as genderqueer or non-binary. These health concerns are unique but informative for how we cover all aspects of Black health. Beyond the binary system, gender-related health in our communities must now face the opportunity of redefinition.

In the path toward respecting gender diversity, we reach a crossroads. At this point, we can allow for gatekept diversity to take us on a smooth, paved path. But that smooth path will lead us to an early cul-de-sac far from our destination. Conversely, co-ordinated diversity will take us on an uncharted oftentimes bumpy terrain toward the favored desti-nation, which is collective prosperity.

What does that journey of respecting gender di-versity look like? What is my responsibility? The journey begins by creating space for challenging conversations on how to redefine masculinity and femininity accompanied by how to define fluidity and nonbinary. As a cisgender male, I can only assist in facilitating conversations regarding the redefinition piece. Like you, I am a willing and eager student who takes a seat, listens, and makes notes regarding the definition piece. In coordinating the space and time for folx to discuss, consider these questions:

1) What steps are you taking to certify that the space is safe and non-judgmental to Black people who do not identify as cisgender masculine/feminine?
2) Who are you talking with (children, adoles-cents/young adults, middle-age, senior citizens)?
3) How much time is used for talking about the past? the present? the future?

4) What opportunities are there for people who identify as gender-nonconforming to speak?

Activity #4

Try using this activity with some of your favorite books and note the level of ease at which you accomplish it.

Practice reading a passage from a book or article where there are a variety of pronouns used. In the passage selected, replace male and female pronouns with a non-gendered pronoun. Start with "they/them/theirs," then re-read the passage and instead use "zim/zer/zeirs." Continue two more times with your own creation of pronouns. Take note of the level of difficulty with each iteration.

In the space below, describe three strategies that will help you become gradually comfortable having conversations about gender diversity.

_____

_____

_____

_____

_____

_____

_____

_____

_____

_____

_____

A coordinated-diversity approach to respecting all facets of gender-related health can assist us in holding space to have conversations about masculinity and femininity that challenge patriarchal notions. These conversations can take place with any age group, with several adjustments needed when going from talking with children to talking with middle-aged adults. Let us begin to compare how these conversation topics appear at different ages and through different diversity approaches.

Children (Ages 4 - 12)

From the age of three, children are aware of the expectations of visible categories such as sex. Because these expectations have been set before birth, children may see them as naturally occurring tendencies that they must obey to avoid punishment or attain rewards. These expectations are boundaries set by adults because it helps them to predict children's behavior, should the smaller humans abide by those standards. They are what form the concept of gender through inferring specific attitudes, beliefs, and behaviors we believe are most representative. These beliefs are often based on the physical appearance or sex anatomy of the child. When children use their physical "gifts" (e.g., for boys, kicking a soccer ball; for girls, building a playhouse) for displaying gender-typical behavior, they are rewarded. When they show behavior typical of the other sex, they are usually chastised for it. Eventually, the cycle of reward and punishment serves to reinforce gender differences.

As we recall, the paradox of gatekeeping is that there is rarely a clear understanding of what one is protecting. Many adults are gatekeeping their communities in a manner that places proverbial brakes on the children who look to live and thrive in the unexplained areas of gender. These areas of gender (i.e., fluidity, internal experiences, and expression) are often personal, with or without the expectations of others.

With time, the construct of gender expands from the demonstration of physical "gifts" in leisure to different responses to puberty. As that construct expands and matures many Black parents may monitor their children closely for "slip-ups" or deviations from expected gender roles. Often, there is no room for assumption that children can experience and express their gender as different from how they or others expect them to present. Their curiosity is viewed as a phase or a response to trauma. Rather than default to these attributions, families, and communities need to begin to learn about gender and its complexity even through the observation of their children's behavior. The behavior of children is just one of many signals to us that gatekeeping is a poor use of our energy.

Coordinated forms of diversity can help us value the concept of gender as a social construct by leading us to become curious about the way we uphold and defy its maintenance in our lives. In the case of the latter, we often violate its supposed "rigidity" in ways that call into question our hope of salvaging the hierarchy we create from it. For example, if we paid attention to the frequency with which children at a very young age appear to be unphased by others' gender variance or self-expression, especially when unsupervised by an adult, it may seem odd. It strikes us unexpectedly that the roles, expectations, and rules are nothing more than straw houses of security that we erect for children. If you don't believe me, rewatch the entire series of Rugrats. That show is filled with gender breaking and rebuilding in its portrayal of babies and toddlers whose world differs significantly from that of their parents, even when in the same room.

Once we begin to accept this notion, we can develop the tools to help coordinate children's changing efforts to understand themselves as a complex form of diversity. Children can feel comfortable associating with stereotypically different forms of leisure without having to be mischaracterized or stigmatized. Even if they are comfortable enough to express that they don't identify with the sex they were assigned at birth, this is a statement based on an informed understanding of self that parents and family may not have the privilege of seeing or knowing. That statement may be an invitation to visit those aspects of the child's identity that the parent was un-aware of but is in the best position to support. Their support can assist the child in further exploring this identity and, eventually, choosing to confirm it or not.

My journey towards accepting myself as a cis-gender male wasn't foreclosed the day I was born. Even growing up within the space of Caribbean pa-triarchal norms, I often found myself mentally painting self-images of Matthew as a girl renamed Mattie. Her image felt right, especially when my fa-vorite Destiny's Child, 702, or Christina Aguilera song came on the radio, and I wanted to dance. I never pictured my girl image dancing to attract atten-tion from boys; mostly, it was to connect with girls and, specifically, my idol girl group or female singer. Whenever my female cousins were visiting and we pretended to be a group, I often envied that they and my sister could form a girl group. On rare occasions, I was made an honorary girl member. Despite the combination of social pressure and time, I eventually chose to identify as a cisgender male through my ac-ceptance of how my body has turned out and the way in which I explored the perceived masculin-ity/femininity of my appearance. Even though Matthew predominates my thinking, I believe that Mattie makes her presence felt when I want to make the beat drop on the dance floor.

As a parent/guardian, you are one of the primary demonstrators of gender to your child, from whom they begin to reference what behaviors and reac-tions are acceptable for their gender. The responsibility falls on you and your family members to be transparent in communicating when something feels uncertain or complicated because parenting comes with questions that are surprisingly difficult to answer. A child who doesn't conform to what you expect doesn't lend you permission to stop conforming to what your role is as a parent: which is to understand your child in the process of raising them. You understand your child so you can raise them, not the other way around. Socializing them to understand the curiosity of the human mind, even if it means exploring gender-atypical behavior, will buffer their self-confidence against the early follies of stigma.

Why are there few children's programs that encourage young boys to learn the skills needed to cook/bake? Why are there few programs for girls that encourage outdoor skills (e.g., setting up a tent, pathfinding)? Or why are there no kids' sci-fi exploration films or shows with a mostly female cast? Maybe one reason is the way we may react to these propositions as older folk and how that gut reaction translates into our support and, ultimately, our children's theories about gender. We must recognize this gut reaction and the factors that form this visceral response. Once we learn how our response to these reactions has limitations, we can begin to remove these limitations to creativity and form practical solutions to the difficulty of raising a child.

The paradigm of coordinated diversity is not meant to be a quick strategy for raising children because it requires more than just a parent/guardian.

When it extends horizontally to aunts/uncles, neighbors, and community leaders, it becomes easier for children to grow up in a community where they are affirmed unconditionally for being the gender that they believe themselves to be. They can understand and accept the curiosity, humility, and compassion that are natural to their upbringing. Coordinated diversity aims to perpetuate the simple notion that diversity isn't segregated. How a child views gender will be influenced by the extent to which we placed limits on what diversity is in our community. As children move through stages of development, we can ensure that newly coordinated approaches to fostering a sense of pride can be waiting for them at each transition.

Youth (Ages 13 - 29)

Just when we thought it couldn't get more complicated, here enters adolescence and young adulthood. The transition from childhood to adolescence to young adulthood is marked by new social factors that influence one's sense of identity. Friends within one's age range become one of the primary sources of social influence, replacing parents and relatives in most situations. Additionally, sexual identity begins to form through the combination of bodily and mental changes to the self. Because of this influx of growth and maturity, it is only appropriate that we address the gender and sexual perspectives together in our comparison of coordinated and gatekeeper approaches to diversity, notwithstanding that gender and sexuality are not the same.

I was fortunate to attend a Catholic high school in the suburbs of Toronto that I felt was culturally transitioning to become more inclusive of people who identified by different gender pronouns and sexual identities. Even with that reality on the horizon (gay-straight alliance student organizations weren't established until a few years after I graduated), I remained closeted in my attraction to the same gender despite the appearance of accepted LGBT staff and students. With same-sex marriage having been made legal the year I began high school; the environment was rife with many teens exploring each other's identities. I befriended and held good relations with people who considered high school to be a "proverbial" science lab where we conducted litmus tests for what beliefs were too acidic, too basic, or lucky number pH 7. When sexuality became the topic of experimentation, the pressure to drift towards polar forms of masculinity prevented many teenage boys from conversations on sexual diversity. Being aware that my sexuality was less typical than most of my friends, I didn't embrace nor express sexuality that was stereotypic of other sexual minorities. What I didn't consider was how the beginning of my sexuality was only one color in a kaleidoscope.

As young people begin to explore their sexuality (yes, it is a voyage!), they are catered to by a market of sexualized images of people their age or older because of the sex appeal this stage of development brings. Sex is fun! There's plenty of it to have and often with little to no strings attached. The freedom to engage in sexual pleasure has always been a topic of controversy as it pertains to the impact that it will have on adolescents and young adults, with more emphasis on the former. If we peer into the world of people from historically devalued identities, we can see that for African Americans, as an example, the debate on sexual liberty, control, and experience can be laden with the ugliest of racist connotations that date back to the Middle Passage of slavery.

Our awareness of conflicting images of sexuality can make the appeal of sex a two-edged sword, especially when we live in a sex-negative culture. Fetishizing certain types of physicality reinforces the sex-negative culture because it creates an image to lust but fear, all at the same time. Young people begin to explore these themes of sex when accompanied by other identities like race or religion the more they are immersed in their social circles and in media depictions of people who look like them.

What can seem like shackles placed on how sexuality can be portrayed in diverse communities may be a moment for us to release from gatekeeping and enter a path of coordination. Instead of trying to measure out what little room we have for authentic self-expression, a method that epitomizes gatekeeper diversity, we can create a room where we understand how sexual expressions positively reflect the diversity in our community and the individual power we have over our sexual identity. In this room, youth who identify as gay, bisexual, demi-sexual, aromantic, and heterosexual can coordinate with one another in sharing the experiences and information they know about themselves without fear of judgment. In this space, we can step back from the pull to be immersed in how we are distorted by existing media and unpack who we truly are, separate from these purported "universals."

How can we develop spaces for the inclusion of youth who identify across the spectrum of sexuality? This question is urgently asked by those who are exhausted with the continuous fight against gatekept forms of diversity. For youth, spaces where sexuality can be expressed freely without harming others are rarely ever considered because we often have people in authority who are not equipped to address the variety and, as a result, view it as threatening to the order. They often imagine worst-case scenarios instead of the best outcomes. Consequently, discussions of sex are limited to avoiding sexually transmitted diseases, HIV, abstinence, and condom use. While well-intended, these topics can be as broaching the conversation of sexual health, the research does not support their efficacy over not discussing sex and sexuality at all. Furthermore, people from sexualities that are not 100% heterosexual find these conversations to be archaic (specific to a time when there were none or few contraceptives).

Applying the paradigm of coordinated diversity to the conversation of sexuality within community requires us to find topics that are both common across sexualities but also open the floor for different perspectives that extend beyond heteronormative inclinations. Instead of only talking about the high prevalence of STIs like HIV in sexually active youth ages 18-29, let's talk about what factors affect the movement from consent to honesty to trustworthiness in a sexual relationship. Let's further unpack how that progression may differ depending on if you are having sex with a person of the same gender or not. Instead of talking about losing one's virginity or sexual debut, let's discuss what forms of sexual pleasure exist outside of penetration (i.e., outercourse). Let's begin to strengthen the consistency of conversations on how masculine stereotypes can affect who is seen as sexually dominant vs submissive. From these discussions, coordinated diversity can allow for its adherents to discuss, brainstorm, and implement plans to bring effective resources to support each individual. Through these conversations, youth who identify along the different spectrums of sexuality will be contributing members and recipients of a supportive network.

Finally, I would be remiss to forgo talking about the physical body in this section on gender and sexual health. The overlap of body image and self-esteem is tremendous at this stage in young-adult development because it offers privilege when a certain shape is lauded. Although youth today are exposed to more body varieties in media than in decades past, the phobia towards bodies that aren't cookie cut into a certain shape betrays the pull towards body positivity. Hence the phrase "more representation doesn't equal better representation". Often, the people who charted the legacy of body positivity are left behind as those whose bodies are "ideal" co-opt the phrasing as solely self-applicable. This lag in attitude change is reflected, for example, in the absence of support for plus-size Black men and women in areas that are traditionally stereotyped for thin or "thicc" people (e.g., modeling, primary or lead acting roles, dance). Clothing proportions that fit the latter leave very few options for plus-size persons who accept their bodies as they are. Combine this limitation with the recognition that when youth begin to identify with a gender that doesn't fit their body, other considerations must be added to the type of support we may need to give them. We have a lot of work to do. These self-imposed limitations may contribute to the persistence of negative attitudes against plus-size cisgender and transgender youth as they venture through adolescence and young adulthood. It is my hope that, at this point in the book, you are getting the picture of how coordinated diversity may change the script for how youth and their adult mentors have conversations.

Activity #5

Take a moment to think of a person within the LGBTQ community whom you know or heard of. If you can't think of one, search online for one person and read their bio. On a piece of paper, draw a Venn Diagram to represent your interests/traits and theirs. In the overlapping part, write down what you believe you share with them. Afterward, draw a line from each interest/trait you jotted down in your circle and connect it to an interest/trait in their circle. The line will represent an interest/trait you would like them to know more about and an interest/trait they have you would like to know more about.

Adults (Ages 30+)

For many of us, the presence of diverse genders and sexual orientations can evoke a multitude of feelings that are dependent on the strength of our attitude on these social categories and the social setting we are currently in. In many of these settings, we are typically in the company of people who share similar views. The strength of having corresponding beliefs is noteworthy because the ease of coordination is simple. Person A, B, and C know each other's strengths and weaknesses; so, their roles are somewhat predefined. When this alignment occurs, you may feel like you have a certain degree of control over the solution because it is what you value the most and you have the help to achieve the outcome.

But what happens when the challenge is unfamiliar, and your setting contains people who do not identify with your previous experiences? I challenge you to step back and imagine how inclusive your vision is of family members who don't identify as male or female or who don't have the same access to the benefits of life as you because they are transgender and can only access affirming treatment through the diagnosis of a mental illness. Like Jacques Lacan posited about thinking of places where we are not located, the level of difficulty in imagining such an environment exists is common. It is a side effect of learning to view a functioning environment based on pre-existing attitudes about people who appear to look or act like us. This learning came from people in places of privilege and power who wanted to keep their grip on the beliefs and unearned assistance that got them to that position. The continuous transfer of these blueprints to "success" can affect the strength with which we gatekeep our communities.

One of the spaces where this type of learning seems to be challenged is in the gendered aspects of Black identity. When we interact with each other, as older adults, the culture associated with Blackness is often recognized by the perceived similar experiences, interests, and life goals. Many in the Black community believe in the quintessential experiences of Blackness that are from an African American lens (e.g., watching The Cosby Show or Good Times, family cookouts, Black barber or salon talk, etc.). Most of these experiences are a product of the construction of culture to survive against slavery and Jim Crow. Often these experiences have come from a male point of view. From exposure to shared experiences, many may create a guarded view of identity by labelling these experiences as not only central but sufficient to the definition of Blackness.

While protective in its function, this lens refuses to consider the differences borrowed from other cultures that are found outside of the construct of Blackness but reflects the diversity of African peoples. As a brief history lesson, many African peoples who were forcibly enslaved were brought to different parts of the Americas. Among those who survived the voyage across the Atlantic, many were forcibly moved or escaped between different ports of South America, the Caribbean, Central America, and the United States. From this history, many traditions within the African American community are a hodgepodge of different traditions that were adopted in the settlements and through interacting with other cultures. Furthermore, add the eventual post-slavery, post-Jim Crow effect of voluntary immigration of African peoples from the former British, French, and Spanish colonies and the incorporation of other cultures into Blackness. The new Blackness in the last half-century hasn't resembled much of the traditional.

Similarly, for many folks who are experiencing adulthood at this special time of human existence, there is a conflict between what has been considered a traditional approach to diversity and the critical thought against an often-monolithic presentation of diversity (i.e., as polarized depictions of people from different cultures). The critical thinking done by people in this age cohort serves to break out of the spaces where thinking was once limited to male-female expectations. It serves to challenge the notion that separatism and the game of respectability politics within diversity do not suffice to create overlapping spaces where coordination between different identities is possible. This critical thinking refuses to accept George Jefferson, Dan Conner, or Tim the Toolman Taylor as the standard of man and, simultaneously, refusing to accept Louise Jefferson, Roseanne Conner, & Fran Fine as the standard of woman. New meaning is the source of their energy to tear down the fragility of gender.

Let's imagine, for a second, you are living single in a small one-bedroom studio apartment. You have your furniture, appliances, closet rack, and the essentials for the space it holds. If you are the loving type, you may decide to allow a family member to come and live with you. You will likely need to factor in how much stuff they will be permitted to bring with them because of the limited space and how long they will be staying. You decide that you will gatekeep what comes and what goes. However, leading up to the days when the move will take place, your family member comes to you with the offer to live in a larger house. Though you know the effort to live in this larger house is greater, there is an opportunity to eventually own a home. What would you do? In this scenario, many of us would decide to take the new option, pack our bags, and give notice to our land-lord.

Our traditional notions of gender are like the current apartment. They are convenient and filled with what we need; but there is a cost that we bear to the use of this space for our enjoyment. Even if the cost is minimal, we are never in a position of ownership over this space. The family member is our socialization method or environment at the moment because we are faced with a test of our capacity to adjust our behavior. When we invite them to live in our apartment, we are socializing via assimilation and accommodation to fit their needs. The new opportunity presented in the larger house creates a new slate where there are new notions of gender, where the family member and us can have a different conversation that does not put our capacities at constant odds with each other. And best of all, there is ownership over self and space in this new environment. With opportunity comes coordination.

Unfortunately, many today do not look at coordinated diversity as the opportunity to own a house that accommodates them and others. People who express and/or defend a train of thinking will defeat the process of moving into that house because they have settled for the singularity and convenience of a one-bedroom studio apartment that barely fits their identity but is best at policing/keeping out "intruders". It is tough to tell how many within our community endorse this thinking because we underestimate the power of situations to affect how we evaluate others and can be susceptible to similar dysfunctional beliefs. But in an effort to develop a coordinated approach to respecting the diversity in our community, what is most important is to expand our collective space where multiple identities are present and thriving. Thriving means to progress and grow despite circumstances. Once we have achieved this state in our community, we can begin to entertain the next stage of diversity: militant diversity.

In the space below, describe three strategies that will help you and others become gradually comfortable having conversations about sexual diversity.

_____

_____

_____

_____

_____

_____

_____

_____

_____

_____

_____

_____

_____

SIX

FROM COORDINATED TO MILITANT DIVERSITY

The purpose of outlining the benefits of coordinated diversity is to position our communities for the long haul in the struggle to achieve the equity we deserve globally and the peace that can ensue afterward. This is a condition that must be met for us to prosper as a social species. I titled this section, militant diversity because it requires empowering ourselves to act strategically in creating a more affirming world at all costs. Creating that affirming world starts with partitioning ourselves to invest in the uplift of many in our community who occupy subjugated identities (e.g., low-income, transgender, women, newcomers, restored citizens). Investment means continuously monitoring the gains and losses of what we place in the trust of others. If, for example, we simply donate money to a cause, that is not an investment; that is a donation. If we donate money but also involve ourselves in the decision-making process of how it is spent and the possible outcomes of its expenditure, we are making an investment. The latter is what militant diversity will require from our community the moment we begin to create plans for prosperity.

Before I go further in explaining what militant diversity is, I will briefly say what it isn't. It is not a movement akin to any traditionally xenophobic philosophy. It isn't a philosophy of anti-immigration or religio-centrism. Many of these movements have traditionally cultivated exclusivity and heterosexist spaces where abstract and diverse thinking is limited. Diversity is seldom appreciated in these places and is dismissed as a product of supremacist thinking. They can be traumatic experiences for many because they are often operated and led by people who have experienced trauma and believe that this is the correct way to surmount it. These groups, while with the best of intentions and with unparalleled enthusiasm for the history and prosperity of their communities, are often taking a gatekeeper approach toward diversity.

Militant diversity is a strategy that receives input from different and diverse minds and produces outputs in multiple spaces and at different times. Each output will be different, but the common denominator is that they will not benefit some people to the exclusion of others. The input received must come from folx in our community who hold multiple identities and interests in collective prosperity. Finally, these inputs must have the potential to be modified when the situation changes so that everyone involved is aware of the importance of the change. This not only prevents us from overvaluing goals that are outdated but helps us feel relevant in the pursuit of collective prosperity.

Because inputs can be filtered through the lens of those who receive them, a standard set of criteria must be established as a guiding part of how we trust what is being given to our community. Coordinated diversity ensures that the information we receive is weighed against this standard. This standard is the goal that encompasses all parties in the coordinator model. Similar to the concept of utilitarianism, where the greatest good affects the greatest number, the standard to which we weigh inputs on plans for our community must account for the majority of people in our communities. It must be trauma-informed, affirming, and flexible. By establishing this standard, our communities will be able to truly heal from the wounds inflicted by society.

CONCLUSION

The connections we establish with others in our community are a product of the affinity we feel toward them. These connections are necessary for safety in times when society is hell-bent on destroying the body and minds of vulnerable populations. The safety afforded by these connections may create a tendency to want to shelter our communities from outsiders to our established culture. Often this is a traumatic response to threats to safety. While adaptive in certain respects, it can lead many in our community to alienate and shun certain forms of diversity. This form of exclusion is gatekeeper diversity because it is a strategy whereby we guard the entry to inclusion. Only certain figures matter. This produces a cycle where societal stigma is reinforced by what criteria are used to select our diversity panel.

I have proposed a paradigm shift by creating a compelling argument for the benefits of coordinated diversity. Coordinated diversity serves to tap into the creativity, ingenuity, and familiarity of diversity within our communities. Diversity within our communities invites others who occupy different and historically devalued identities to be affirmed without having to occupy a separate community. With further separation, gatekept diversity continues to hold its grip on how we operate in pursuit of collective prosperity. Coordinated diversity doesn't require us to come together and put away our differences. Rather, like the Remote Associates Test, we need to take a naive-student approach to learning about the vastness of our communities, without hostility.

Coordinated diversity will not happen overnight because it will require many to read this book and endorse its philosophy of redefining self and community. Each of the areas of health highlighted in the previous sections - environment, gender, and sexuality - is often the subject of contested debates that do not accomplish much. But the authors are confident that the words written will make an impression on people of diverse experiences in our communities. We hope that reading this book and participating in its activities can create several stepping-stones toward the destination of a redefined self and community.

MEET THE AUTHORS

DR. JESSE SANDERS
Dr. Jesse Sanders has his Ph.D. from Metropolitan Christian University and is known to many as Dr. Redefined, Your Redefining Mental Health Counselor, Public Speaker, Conversationalist, best- selling author, influencer, and public figure. In addition, Dr. Sanders is a single and co-parenting father of his two beautiful daughters, Brianna and Brielle. He is innovative and does not operate with boundaries. For more than 20 years, Dr. Sanders has led people to find tenacity and strength to change their circumstances through positive self-inquiry and actions. Providing therapeutic and social support to individuals and families who are living at the intersections of multiple oppressions, Dr. Sanders initiates relevant conversations to redefine lives in a radical way.

DR. MATTHEW WILMOT

Dr. Matthew Wilmot is a community health educator at the Midwest AIDS Training and Education Center, located at Ohio State University's Wexner Medical Center. Prior to this appointment, Dr. Matt completed his Ph.D. in psychology from the University of Waterloo where he researched the topics of institutional prejudice, social perception, STEM culture, and health behaviors. He has given talks on the subject of critical race theory, diversity, and mental health on numerous panels (Black Ph.D. Network, Cocktails and Conversations, and Exodus Nation). As a community health educator, Dr. Matt orients toward providing seminars on HIV and COVID-19 to underserved communities in Columbus (e.g., African, LGBTQIA, and first-generation American). His education and experiences privilege him with the ability to speak on a number of topics, found on his website at www.heydrmatt.com. Dr. Matt is a champion for channeling existing diversity into a pedagogy that facilitates thinking beyond our own perspectives to the inclusion of others. When not trying to save the world, Dr. Matt loves to read a good book, play piano, speak French and Swahili, and share cute photos of dogs. Dr. Matt is a native of the best city in the world, Toronto, Canada, though he currently resides with his partner, Zach, in Columbus, Ohio.

www.ingramcontent.com/pod-product-compliance
Lightning Source LLC
Chambersburg PA
CBHW060325130626
46553CB00003B/921